18 Way to Put up Your E-book on Amazon Kindle.

Step .1 Sonstructing the book:

Step .2 Start it up.

Step .3 The way to submit Your personal e-book on Kindle

Step 4: prepare

Step 5: test

Step 6: Examine greater study

Step 7. High Yield Checking or wireless bills

. Step 8: Condo wi-fits

Step 9:Selling records products

Step 10:Get professional help

Step 11:Read more study

Step 12:New Amazon Kindle book shows how forex investors can promote.

Step 13:How to: post Your weblog on the Amazon Kindle

Step 14:Amazon announces virtual forex for use with Kindle wi-fireplace, Appstore

Step 15:How Amazon Kindle unlimited Scammers Wring large cash From Phony Books

Step 16:How to Hustle Kindle limitless

Step 17: What's Amazon doing?

if you're seeking out a manner to self-put up your very own book on the Kindle, it is fairly easy. right here's the step-by-step method of making your writing to be had to the Kindle hundreds.

Your ebook shouldn't tour that rocky of a road on its manner to book.

Amazon makes it a piece of cake so that it will set an e-book free at the Kindle e-reader platform.

Step .1 Sonstructing the book:

• Write your book in Microsoft phrase and keep it as a .document wi-fine wireless. skip the .rtf and .docx codecs. They don't play nicely with the Kindle.

• pay attention to how you format your text. Bolding, italicizing, and indenting are not any trouble, however, steer clear of bullets, headers, footers, and fancy fonts.

• Any images you use need to be in a .jpeg format with center alignment. take into account that the Kindle can most effective show images in grayscale.

• thoughts your grammar and spelling. whilst you get them wrong, it,s embarrassing.

Saving in Filtered HTML format: once the entirety appears accurate, pick wi-fi, keep as, web page, Filtered (*HTM &*HTML). clean sufwiwireless.

the usage of Mobipocket writer is a bit of software program that will turn your Filtered HTML wi-file wireless into an e-book to sell thru Amazon. it is simplest well suited with pcs walking windows 2000/XP or extra. There are not any solutions given on Amazon's wi-legitimate website for those walking OSX, so wi-fi pal going for walks the proper working device and download the software right here.

Step .2 Start it up.

• select "HTML wi-fi" from the segment "Import from a present report."

• Browse to the HTML wireless and press "Import."

• this can open the book enhancing feature. click on "cowl picture."

• click on "add a cowl image" and browse your wi-fi to wi-find the ebook cowl.

• pick your ebook cover and click "update" to store your cowl.

- pick "construct" from the Menu.
- on the build web page, click on "construct."
- once whole, the message "construct wi-fi wireless" will seem.
- click on the circle next to "Open folder containing ebook" and choose "adequate."
- The wireless has been stored in .% layout on your My wireless/My guides folder.

cover your book and use Kindle Previewer will show you precisely what the reader will see whilst he reads your e-book. download it right here and use it to open your .% wireless. Did you seize a mistake? exchange it for your unique Microsoft word document and undergo the equal technique new wireless above to output a new .% wi-fine wireless.

Get published after your happy wireless with your wi-finished product, upload your .% wi-fi here. After getting into to your pricing and royalty statistics, click "keep and put up." Your ebook will appear for sale in the Amazon e-book shop within 24-forty eight hours. Amazon gives you 70 percent of all sales. inform your buddies to buy it and tell John Grisham to devour his heart out.

alternatives Apple is the other huge participant making a foray into helping authors self-publish their ebooks. Their iBooks platform makes it a snap to shop for ebooks to read on your iPhone, iPod touch, or iPad, but getting your ebook into their market is appreciably trickier.

earlier than even wireless your ebook for their consideration, you want a manuscript in ePub format, a 13-digit ISBN, validation against ePubCheck 1.zero.wi-five, a US Tax wi-fi, a valid iTunes shop account, and an Intel-based Mac strolling Leopard or higher.

None of these things are possible, however, we're much greater impressed with how trustworthy and reachable the identical system is through Amazon.in case you want to provide iBooks a try, the manner starts offevolved here.

Step .3 The way to submit Your personal e-book on Kindle

I have been writing my tech weblog virtual thought for about 8 years, and in that time I've come across loads of websites that offer records in addition to remedy actual troubles.

some of these websites, or web apps — like Pixlr (picture editor), Creately (diagrams creator) and home Styler (three-D dressmaker) — are almost as effective as their desktop cousins, together with GIMP and Visio.

I wanted to position these "gems of the internet" in a reference ebook and turned into confronted with selections: I could either move down the conventional direction and create a print version of the ebook, or take the opposite less complicated alternative of self-publishing in a digital layout. The latter made extra experience because of e-books. There aren't any upfront expenses.

here's some advice for any wannabe authors looking to do likewise:

wherein to publish?

There are numerous platforms for publishing and dispensing eBooks. The maximum popular is obviously Amazon's Kindle store, but there's also the iBookstore of Apple, Barnes & Noble's corner store and the Sony Reader keep, amongst others.

The iBookstore calls for a U.S. Tax identiwiwireless even for global publishers, but you can nevertheless get your e-book listed in Apple's market through third-birthday celebration aggregators like Lulu or Smashwords, who take a fee in keeping with the sale. The iBookstore continues to be now not extensively to be had in India — as an example, you can handiest download unfastened ebooks from the iBooks app, however, none of the paid titles are to be had. Kindle, then again, is worldwide and, wi-fi wireless of all, gives studying apps for all structures, so even non-Kindle customers can experience the ebook on their desktops and mobile telephones. I decided to go the Kindle manner.

Step 4: prepare

Preparing the ebook is simply the usage of commonplace equipment like Microsoft phrase or Google Docs. It's just like writing a regular wi-file wireless but avoid complicated styles. keep on with not unusual fonts like Arial or Times New Roman, don't experiment with colorings, keep your pictures centered (don't align them left or proper) and don't upload headers or footers as they're not supported via the Kindle. Even tables and bulleted lists may not look right, so avoid them if possible.

once your document is prepared, shop it in HTML layout (phrase offers that option) and then use the loose Mobipocket writer device to transform your record right into a Kindle wi-record. You need to additionally create a six hundred×800 picture in order to act as a cowl for your ebook. remember to use large fonts due to the fact the Amazon keep will most effective show a thumbnail photograph of the cover and the ebook title need to nonetheless be readable at that reduced length.

Step 5: Examine greater study

Your extra wi-fits move(s) can be something you are actively worried in: aside commercial enterprise, as an example, or creative undertaking like writing a blog. it could additionally be passive income—this is, regular wi-fits that does not require plenty of protection—which includes lease you get from your private home or royalties from e-book sales. investment hobby and dividends also have the capability to provide a more movement of wi-fi.

This guide focuses on easy techniques for passive wi-fi streams you can get started out with proper away, on the grounds that they have a tendency to be the most wireless approaches to get more from your initial time and money funding.*

Step 6. High Yield Checking or wireless bills

An easy way to make your cash work wi-ficult is to enhance the interest charge on your wi-fi. The common wi-fi or money market account today yields much less than 1% interest, but we can do better—without taking on greater risk.

although excessive-yield wi-fi banks don't generate as a lot hobby as they used to, online banks nonetheless generally tend to generate higher hobby charges than traditional brick-and-mortar accounts. To compare online financial institution quotes, test Bankrate's account wi-finder tools, localized on your location.

discover a wireless excessive-yield wi-financial saving wireless account

personal-wirelessnance blog Get wealthy Slowly went looking for a high-yield online wireless account and...

Step 7: Read more examine

some other choice no longer frequently discussed: high yield or reward checking bills, typically offered by way of smaller banks and credit unions and still insured by using the FDIC. you will soar through a few hoops, like making a minimal variety of debit card transactions in line with month, but in going back you may earn extra than four times the common measly hobby price. One source for wireless those sorts of debts is Deposit debts (or simply do a Google search for "praise checking debts" or "excessive yield checking money owed" + your kingdom).

You won't get wealthy by using switching to a higher-yielding checking or wi-financial saving wireless account, however, you may turn out to be with more wi-financial saving wireless. each dollar you earn and keep will generate extra hobby income. (greater volatile investments are past the scope of this newsletter, but a source for starting buyers is the Investor's Clearinghouse, a non-wireless which offers equipment and articles for the entirety from bond fundamentals to pinnacle investment scams.)

Step 8: Condo wi-fits

regularly—or, at least earlier than the actual estate bust—a great deal advice about generating wealth involved a number of real estate speculation or flipping of homes (shopping for wi-fixer-uppers or undervalued residences after which promoting them for a good deal higher). after all, a number of the maximum distinguished wirelessly wealthy celebrities, like Donald Trump, made their fortunes with the aid of making an investment in real property.

however, making an investment in actual property is an awful lot riskier than it was once, calls for numerous work wireless the proper property and qualifying/deciding to buy it, and commonly additionally comes with plenty of headaches. Being a landlord regularly method managing tough wireless or deadbeat tenants, luxurious belongings repairs, and other elements that make managing this form of investment less wireless than it sounds.

you could nonetheless hire area or equipment you already very own, but, without any additional investment or lots hassle. previously cited Zilok lets you list all sorts of gadgets to rent—the entirety from equipment to fixtures to cabins. one in each of my pals has made a few side wi-fi renting out professional-grade wi-fi system he bought for more than one preceding projects. you can even lease out a top parking spot through Park Circa.

if you have a spare room in your home, attic space or a basement, renting out that a part of your own home is some other way to make greater from what you have already were given. you can decide a fair rental charge to your region with Zillow's Rent Zestimate. (you will nonetheless cope with all the landlord, or roommate, hassles, however, it is less of a sizeable funding than trying to end up a real estate tycoon.)

 decide an honest condo fee with Zillow's rent Zestimates

whether you are a landlord (or an "unintentional landlord" way to the economic system) or a...

read greater read 3. putting Your expertise on the net

there is a ton of data online for the blogging model for generating passive wi-fits. This makes wi-finding wireless straightforward information extra wi-hard.

The most effective path is to start running a blog about something you're very obsessed with — widgets, for instance — and add affiliate hyperlinks to distinct widget stores (e.g., via the Amazon buddies software) in your blog posts (with wi-find word that these are ad-subsidized links). See our newbie's manual to creating an internet website online or other blogging sources to get began growing the web site itself.

 the way to Make an internet website online: The entire novice's guide

wi-fi week we taught you a way to make a website from beginning wi-fi, such as wireless a dependable...

study more read

There are brilliant many affiliate programs you can get started with, along with Google AdSense, fee Junction, and LinkShare. if you're geared up to enter the extraordinary extensive global of including sales-producing advert links for your website, Schuff recommends IM record Card for wi-fi critiques of diverse packages and search for 9aaf3f374c58e8c9dcdd1ebf10256fa5, truthful bloggers who write about this subject matter.

perhaps the maximum essential thing whilst you're doing that is that you handiest embed the links to products or services you would certainly endorse to others. most of the people like product guidelines from people they consider (you, the blogger), but we are all cautious of shills.

Step 9:Selling records products

Is there a book in you? every kind of specialized knowledge or skill has the capacity to be packaged as an e-book, ebook, CD, DVD, sport, poster and/or many other codecs. Mitchell York, who writes about entrepreneurship for approximately.com, says that information merchandise does not should be modern to be of a price. The internet makes selling statistics merchandise (e.g., the way to develop the largest tomatoes inside the Northeast) much less high priced to provide and market. it is pretty smooth to publish your ebook on Kindle or Apple's iBooks.

the way to submit Your ebook on Amazon Kindle

in case you're seeking out a way to self-submit your personal e-book at the Kindle, it is...

read more read

different varieties of passive prowiwireless consist of royalties from images, paintings, patents, or other highbrow belongings you could license out.

a way to Get started out

To locate wireless greater possibilities for you, take into account: What do you very own or recognize that others may need to pay you for? What are you most interested in? seek advice from buddies and own family to discover methods you may practice your wi-fi abilities closer to both passive wi-fi (e.g., a static website with ad revenue or a self-published ebook) or lively wi-fi (a part-time consulting commercial enterprise).

Step 10:Get professional help

Schuff says that the most critical advice she will give is to create a stable basis by means of getting help from a capable professional in putting in place your accounting device and, if needed, business structure. whether or not you're an entrepreneur or someone simply searching out a few cash on the aspect, make certain to music your development:

Your monetary e-books and records are not only a bunch of numbers. They tell you how your commercial enterprise is doing. whilst you recognize what the numbers are telling you, you'll recognise which of your services and products are the maximum wi-fiprowiwireless, whether your cash go with the flow is sufwiwireless to pay your bills, and what sort of you may have the funds for to spend on system and materials.

if you have any recommendations or revel in to proportion approximately setting your money in motion, please proportion them with us inside the remarks.

* those thoughts all are based totally on the assumption that you have the fundamentals down wi-first: a healthful emergency fund and your debt paid off.photo with the aid of HarshLight

Step-by means of-Step guide to a wholesome Emergency Fund

An emergency fund might also look like a luxury in the midst of a recession, however in case you do not have...

Step 11:Read more study

Sheryl Schuff is the go-to person at the net sellers Circle for questions on accounting, e-bookkeeping, and QuickBooks and serves on the panel of specialists on the worldwide wi-fi of Solopreneurs. you may wireless her blog at SherylSchuff.com and observe her on Twitter @SherylSchuff.

you may contact or comply with Melanie Pinola, the author of this publish, on Twitter.

Step 12:New Amazon Kindle book shows how forex investors can promote.

Their buying and selling information and Make a Passive pro wireless

The Dewi-definitive ebook on Turning an interest in currency exchange into a lucrative commercial enterprise opportunity is now to be had in a digital form for use with Kindle; The e-book is "the way to start Your own forex sign provider" and it is Now to be had at Amazon

VILNIUS, LITHUANIA / ACCESSWIRE / July 1, 2015 / Written by Rimantas Petrauskas, the e-book gives a step by step manual for folks that see the opportunity for achievement by means of starting and developing their own sign service. it's like having a person pointing out ability pitfalls and leading alongside the course to a wonderful learning wireless.

The book has been in the marketplace for about a year. It has generated interest and sold loads of copies in ebook shape. but this e-book is simply too valuable for the masses to miss it due to the fact it's miles most effective supplied and is to be had in the print layout. So creator Rimantas Petrauskas determined to provide it to a much wider audience by imparting it in the digital layout similarly to the print model. this will make the commercial enterprise possibility this e-book outlines accessible to tens of millions more humans international. this could make a precious addition to the summer season analyzing listing of entrepreneurs and others with an interest in currency trading who need to understand the way to promote trading signals.

The print version of "a way to start Your own foreign exchange signal provider" has been properly obtained internationally. people interested in the worldwide currency market have been drawn to it because of the treasured records it affords. such a lot of people expressed an interest in the ebook that it rose as excessive as number 4 on the listing of the pinnacle one hundred ebooks within the forex class. presenting the e-book inside the virtual format and generating a Kindle model will actually wireless human beings worldwide which are seeking out a moneymaking enterprise opportunity.

whilst the ebook is an exciting examine for everybody with a hobby in an impartial enterprise, it's of speciwiwireless interest to currency buyers. Many foreign money buyers are looking for an easy way to start their own enterprise on this interesting field. The e-book gives a smooth to follow guide for moving into wi-the wireless. for plenty of currency traders, this ebook has the exact statistics they need to help them begin their own buying and selling indicators selling a business. with the aid of imparting a virtual model, the author is capable of delivering many extra currency buyers easy and convenient access to the information.

Rimantas Petrauskas is uniquely certified to write down "the way to start Your own forex signal carrier." the writer has many years of enjoying the area and has played many roles in the enterprise. He has spent a number of years as a forex trader. He is likewise an entrepreneur that has created several a hit companies. What has given him wi-finitely unique wireless insights into the industry is his paintings as a programmer. Petrauskas has been concerned in growing effective software for use in foreign exchange signal transport and foreign exchange for greater than 6 years. He has helped several customers by way of growing masses of trading robots. he's now giving the majority get right of entry to this valuable statistics.

For human beings which might be interested in offering facts on trades to potential clients and beginning an independent signal service, there may be one piece of software program they want. That software is featured in "how to begin Your very own foreign exchange sign provider." inside the ebook it's miles known as the far-off trade Copier. The name has given that been wi-fi to the sign Magician software. it is one of the simplest ways to offer customers with the statistics they need to achieve success while making trades in the forex marketplace. The software program increases their knowledge of a way to take gain wireless of the possibilities within the forex marketplace.

For someone inquisitive about the foreign money market and thinking about establishing an impartial signal carrier, the book presents the data wanted in ebook shape or on Kindle with the aid of touring Amazon.

Step 13:How to: post Your blog on the Amazon Kindle

There are a few interesting matters you may do with a Kindle. one in all them is the potential to enroll in and study your favorite blogs at the pass. In fact, this is how my mother reads my weblog posts - via Mashable on the Kindle.

it is a smooth and on-the-pass way to study your preferred blogs, however, it becomes best available to 3 excessive-prowl-file web guides - as a minimum, till today, whilst Amazon launched its Kindle Publishing for Blogs software. Now that you know approximately this system, your subsequent question is probably: how do I get my blog syndicated to thousands of Kindles?

Signing up for Kindle Publishing for Blogs

So there are several caveats to beginning with the brand new Kindle blog service. First element: you have to create a separate account for the program. Your current Amazon or Kindle account is not enough. You want to enter wi-financial records, consisting of your tax id range and bank account records. you can sign on for this system if you're not of the U.S., however, there are numerous problems involved (factors below).

as soon as you've got a Kindle Publishing account, you simply have to provide your blog's RSS feed, an outline, a screenshot, and more descriptive records and voila! Your weblog's content material will soon be on the Kindle (after it passes Amazon's approval method).

Receiving compensation

even as your blog may be on a Kindle, you probably might not make a whole lot of cash. allow's speak approximately numbers. First, you don't get to choose to price - Amazon does, based on what it believes is honest. this means $0.ninety nine or $1.ninety nine in step with the month for most blogs. there is no way to distribute your blog without spending a dime, both.

also essential: you handiest get 30% of the subscription revenue. for that reason in case your weblog is going for $zero.ninety nine cents and a thousand people subscribe to it through the Kindle, you're now not going to make $990, but as a substitute $297. For fundamental publishers, this isn't a prime source of pro wireless, however, is higher than nothing.

global publishers can most effective acquire their wi-finances through a U.S. check, that can include full-size fees to cash.

blog distribution at the Kindle: is it really worth it?

here's the truth: you are no longer going to make a ton of money from the Kindle, as a minimum for now. it's a pleasing way to examine blogs on-the-go, even though snapshots are black-and-white and video is non-existent. We do not have numbers on how many people read blogs on the Kindle, but we wager it isn't an amazing amount.

yet the greater techniques distribution in your content material, the higher. We do wish that the Kindle offers content material creators a bigger piece of the pie, though. this will make Kindle weblog publishing a more feasible alternative.

Amazon's new Kindle Oasis is the quality e-reader (a variety of) money should buy

a few years in the past, the top rate e-reader turned into an oxymoron. For Amazon, Kobo and Barnes and Noble, pills have been the clean excessive give up of the studying marketplace, with the color touchscreen and full app shops. For a moment, it regarded inevitable that e-ink devices would soon come to be obsolete.

however, the products by no means went away. There had been simply too many blessings that LCDs couldn't replicate: weeks lengthy battery lifestyles, outside studying and mitigation of eye fatigue. E-readers would generally outlive studying drugs, whilst the hitherto unparalleled top class started to emerge. whilst the Kindle Oasis debuted losing wireless year, it became clear that Amazon had the class on lock-down.

The premium class stays a niche, of a path. The new version of the reader is priced between $270 and $350, which means you can get 3 access-degree Kindles for the rate of the cheapest version of the Oasis. The wi-advantages are clean, of a path, from a far greater strong build with a better-res, large display to Audible capability and, for the primary time on a Kindle, waterproof-fine.

It handily grabs the title of the wireless Kindle ever and is a pretty solid contender for great committed e-reader ever. the brand new Oasis walks that eternal e-reader tightrope among forced simplicity and new capabilities — and basically succeeds. It's an ambitious acknowledgment at the tenth anniversary of the authentic Kindle that the class is still going moderately robust. And yeah, it's gonna price you.

Rear bumper

however wi-ficientwireless of that e-ink stuff. lets without a doubt start things off by talking about the back, due to the fact e-reader backs are important and no person honestly talks about them. The lower back changed into one of the matters that kept me coming again to corner readers — Barnes and Noble actually put a few notions into them. they may be, in spite of everything, the part of the reader your hand is in contact with greater than any other. You'll likely spend hours a week touching the issue — many, many hours, if you're the kind of reader who's willing to spend ~$three hundred on a device.

The Oasis has an aluminum again — the kind you'll wireless on premium smartphones, every different year, while the employer determined now not to go together with glass. It's night time and day in phrases of premium experience, in comparison to the same old plastic backing you'll wi-fi wireless on maximum readers. It appears loads nicer, too, but possibilities are you're no longer going to spend a variety of time searching on the brushed aluminum backing.

There's additionally that unsightly lip. I'm no longer in love with the look of the bump — a compromise the employer made in trying to make the relaxation of the tool "as close to paper as viable." however electronics innards (wi-fiscally the battery) need an area to stay, and Amazon essentially bunched all of them up in a single corner in order to distribute the majority of the reader's weight at once into the hand.

In concept, the bump also gives the hand an area to grip onto the lower back of the tool, though it's a chunk shallow and too clean to really get a lot of traction. additionally, in case you emerge as choosing one in every of Amazon's proprietary instances, it essentially negates the uneven backing, slotting in proper next to the bump.

lower back to the buttons.

the whole thing that's vintage is new once more. So it's likely no wonder that Amazon lowers back to bodily web page-flip buttons after years of swearing them off. It's in all likelihood the thing that's most irritated me about e-reader layout during the last several years. Touchscreens have stepped forward at the devices, however, they're nowhere near the responsiveness or tactile pride of clicking that button. but producers together decided to kill them, probably for aesthetic motives.

like the battery bump on the opposite, software happily trumps looks this day trip, and huge buttons have been covered amongst a black expanse of a side bezel. They've got wi-fi click on to them and are plenty responsive. wireless of all, they make it plenty easier to examine with one hand, if you spend a whole lot of time striking off a subway ballot — or, you realize, sitting on a seaside with a Corona in the other hand.

The inclusion of an accelerometer is prime right here — in contrast to earlier Kindles, the Oasis has actually wireless facets, with the buttons positioned closest to the hand protecting it. due to the fact the Kindle knows which aspect is up, it's capable of turn the display screen orientation, so it is able to be used right- or left-exceeded. Amazon even went to date as getting rid of the brand from the front of the tool, so there's no clear top or backside.

That side bezel provides a fair quantity to the Oasis's floor vicinity — that's already quite good sized, way to the organization's decision to add a complete inch to the display. Amazon's not the first corporation to transport beyond the same old six-inch display (in truth, this isn't even the first time it's accomplished so), but it's still a reasonably radical change, as a way as these items move. The complete industry regarded to together determine to transport off six inches a while back.

by way of Amazon's depend, that equals out to approximately 30 percentage greater words according to a page. That, ultimately, approach much less page turning, of a path. extra display area additionally theoretically way the device must be higher for such things as comics — though, as I've formerly mentioned, e-ink technologically hasn't genuinely made plenty development inside the wi-fi numerous years.

sure the three hundred PPI decision is a brilliant development, however, matters are simply too laggy and refreshes take too lengthy to genuinely experience something with quite a few arts. believe me, I've attempted. regardless of manga, that is drawn and revealed in black and white, it's just now not going to occur. The Kindle is a text shipping tool.

the most important information right here, but, is almost clearly waterproowirelessng. Amazon becomes at the back of the curve, as Kobo's been offering the functionality for some time now, however it's a great addition though. positive, it seems a piece silly, but for those instances, you get caught inside the rain (or spill your piña colada, for that remember), it's a godsend. And don't underestimate the wide variety of folks that examine inside the bathtub.

The Oasis is rated at IPX8, which means it could be submerged up to a few meters for 30 minutes. In different phrases, it may cope with a dunk in the tub, but don't take the element scuba diving. You'll wi-find a better way to examine Jules Verne to the moray eels in your lifestyles. The circulate to water-proof the device changed into probably one of the reasons the employer opted to forgo the headphone jack.

The Kindle's already been thru that rodeo earlier than. And except, with the headphone jack, which has already being fought on other fronts, Amazon just opted to move the Bluetooth direction while it came to onboard audio. Heck, like the iPhone earlier than it, the Oasis's positioning as a top class device does make it much more likely that capacity users will already personal a pair of well-matched headphones.

The syncing manner is pretty honest, and Amazon's WhisperSync era means ebooks pick up kind of wherein you left off as you toggle among text and Audible audiobook. It's a neat characteristic, even though. however if we're assuming users have Bluetooth headphones, it's in all likelihood now not too large a bounce to imagine they already have a phone, as properly — in which case, there possibly aren't too many instances whilst it makes extra feel to pay attention to the audio ebook model of an e-book on the Kindle.

a pleasing side wi-fit of the flow to audio e-books is Amazon's wi-first storage increase in some time. The employer has never been tons on the expandable garage and has in large part pointed to cloud syncing when it comes to building a large library, but the addition of audio e-books necessitates a boom in the onboard area. the base model has been doubled to 8GB, and things move as much as 32GB, which translates to a variety of e-books.

A decade of Kindling

There are, of a route, sure advantages to being in the sport for as long as Amazon. year through a year, the organization has introduced new capabilities, which includes the aforementioned WhisperSync, the contextual search of X-Ray and integrations with its social analyzing providing, GoodReads. The latter still seems like a chunk of an afterthought, although that's possibly in service of making sure that the studying experience doesn't get slowed down with too many distractions.

though, of a route, it's nonetheless gifted from some of the menus, offering up direct get admission to the organization's 7451f44f4142a41b41fe20fbf0d491b7 keep. because despite the fact that the Oasis is still priced as a top rate tool, content material continues to be king. And as such, the business enterprise doesn't make it in particular clean to head outdoor of the store. The reality that the reader doesn't do ePub wireless is going to continue to be a deal breaker for many potential users, myself covered.

There are, however, some wireless under-the-radar additions, as properly. There are more font length alternatives and additional levels of bolding. The textual content can also be "ragged proper" aligned, just like what you wireless in a general book, in which the right margin isn't uniform, so the textual content doesn't need to be spaced out to compensate.

There's additionally an option to invert the colors, with white textual content on a black history for users with mild sensitivity — though Amazon tells me a number of testers have located it to be less difwiwireless on the eyes is preferred. the brand new larger display also brings the potential to increase icons for the visually impaired.

unique version

The e-reader category hasn't advanced as quickly as different patron electronics, because of each a loss of competition and limitations of the distance. That stated, Amazon's still supplying up masses of desire inside its own portfolio, even as companies like Kobo are retaining a few semblances of choice.

The Oasis doesn't have too much opposition to the excessive stop. The Kobo air of secrecy One is probably as near as it receives at $230, but the new Kindle is an all-around more top rate revel in. At $270, it's centered at a niche of a niche, but in 2017, it's without difwiwireless the wireless excessive-stop e-reader enjoy for those who want to sing out the notion-fications and read the day away.

Step 14:Amazon announces virtual forex for use with Kindle wi-fireplace, Appstore

Amazon has introduced their very very own digital forex for use with their famous Kindle wi-fi series of capsules and Amazon Appstore. they're calling it — watch for it — Amazon coins. The virtual cash will enter flow with the purpose to drive monetization for builders, permitting customers to buy apps, games, and in-app bonuses beginning this could.

For starters, Amazon is gifting away "tens of millions of dollars' worth" of the brand new foreign money to spark their digital economic system, but the goal is to get users spending real international coins on the digital dough. It's a win-win for Amazon and builders. money stays inside the Kindle wi-fireplace ecosystem and devs earn similar to they might normally.

developers have until April 25th to put together their apps for Amazon cash. Pricing info and trade charges have not begun to be disclosed.

Introducing Amazon cash

Coming in may, Amazon cash is a brand new virtual forex for buying apps, video games, and in-app objects on Kindle wi-fireplace

Amazon cash is an easy manner for Kindle wireless clients to spend money on builders' apps in the Amazon Appstore, providing app and recreation builders some other great possibility to power wireless, downloads and growth monetization even in addition

Amazon will supply clients tens of millions of bucks' really worth of Amazon coins to apply on developers' apps within the Amazon Appstore—apps and video games should be submitted and accredited through April 25 to be prepared when Amazon Coins arrive in clients' debts

SEATTLE—February wi-fi, 2013—(NASDAQ: AMZN)—Amazon these days introduced another new way for app and sports builders to make money on Kindle wireless—introducing Amazon cash—the new virtual currency for buying apps, video games and in-app gadgets on Kindle wi-fine wireless. Amazon Coins is an easy manner for Kindle wi-fi wireless clients to spend money on the Amazon Appstore, supplying app and game developers another vast opportunity to force wi-fitrafwiwireless, downloads and growth monetization. when Amazon coins launch inside the U.S. this may, Amazon will supply customers tens of hundreds of thousands of dollars' well worth of unfastened Amazon coins to spend on builders' apps on Kindle wireless in the Amazon Appstore. Amazon may also make it brief and easy for customers to buy extra Amazon coins the use of their Amazon debts.

Amazon Appstore builders will earn their widespread 70 percent sales percentage when clients make purchases using Amazon Coins. developers with apps and games presently within the Amazon Appstore for the U.S. don't want to do anything with their apps to capitalize on this new opportunity. developers not but within the Amazon Appstore must put up their apps quickly—most effective apps submitted and approved by means of April 25 could be equipped whilst Kindle wi-fi customers have Amazon cash to spend across the Amazon Appstore. developers can examine greater approximately Amazon cash today at http://www.amazon.com/amazon-coins.

"builders retain to report higher conversion charges on Amazon compared to different systems," stated Paul Ryder, vice president of Apps and games for Amazon. "Now we've got another new way to help builders attain even extra of our thousands and thousands of clients. Amazon cash offers customers a smooth way to spend money on builders' apps on Kindle wi-wireless in the Amazon Appstore—and we're giving clients tens of hundreds of thousands of bucks in Amazon coins to get commenced. developers who aren't yet within the Amazon Appstore will need to ensure their apps had been submitted and authorized by way of April 25 so that they're equipped for customers to start spending their Amazon Coins."

"We've already determined that the common sales consistent with a person on Amazon is higher than other Android structures," stated Keith Shepherd, CEO of Imangi Studios. "We're very enthusiastic about the monetization opportunity with Amazon's new virtual forex."

"all of us acknowledges Amazon's fulwiwireless in the e-commerce international – now the Amazon Appstore has become a primary participant in the cell app marketplace," stated Misha Lyalin, ZeptoLab's CEO. "Amazon's new digital currency is designed to open new possibilities for builders and make things wi-ficult for clients. that is a wi-first-rate instance of app store innovation and we need to assist it."We've been extremely thrilled with how well our games monetize on Amazon," stated Michael Grobe, leader monetary Ofwirelesscer of GameCircus. "We're very excited about the release of Amazon's new virtual currency."

Amazon coins are the present day in a series of new functions and offerings for developers that make Amazon the most whole quit-to-end surroundings for constructing, monetizing and marketing their apps and games. recent announcements include:• In-App shopping for Mac, laptop, and net-primarily based games, enabling builders to let customers use their Amazon accounts to purchase virtual items and currencies from video games on the one's platforms

• recreation Circle, which includes abilities like Achievements, Leaderboards, buddies, and Whispersync for syncing games throughout gadgets, and ends in better engagement with video games

• recreation join, which we could builders marry the benefit and protection of purchasing on Amazon with the ease of having virtual items delivered at once to clients' recreation money owed

• A/B trying out, a service that enables builders to improve app functionality, keep clients and increase monetization

• Adobe AIR Native Extensions, which makes it simple for Adobe Flash builders to feature In-App buying and sport Circle features to their apps and games

• Amazon cell App SDK Eclipse Plugin (beta) lets in builders to hastily and reliably integrate Amazon APIs into their Android tasks, rushing up improvement and cutting down on task setup time developers can get began at the Amazon cell App Distribution Portal (https://developer.amazon.com/welcome.html).

Step 15:How Amazon Kindle unlimited Scammers Wring large cash From Phony Books

limitless e-books, what could go wrong? Thomas Lohnes/Getty photographs

What if rip-off artists could make heaps of dollars publishing unfastened, faux e-books that human beings are tricked into beginning however in no way examine? It looks as if that's happening.

Amazon created Kindle limitless, a Netflix for ebooks, that's handing over indie authors sales and readers. however, it turns out that the manner it really works may also have créated an opportunity for scammers to scouse borrow wi-fi from real writers producing real works.

On the brilliant side, Amazon isn't spying on Kindle users as they study. That's a tiny bit of correct information inside the discouraging story approximately hacking a monthly pool of a few million dollars which means loads to 7451f44f4142a41b41fe20fbf0d491b7 writers, however, works out to small exchange for an organization that broke $one hundred billion in revenue for the primary time the last yr.

case in point: Walter Jon Williams has been publishing ebooks since 1984, back whilst Amazon founder Jeff Bezos was still working closer to commencement at Princeton. As time has exceeded, he's been bringing out-of-print ebooks returned into stream digitally. In March, he becomes jogging a paid promotion on his title Metropolitan (which heat the beginning posted with HarperCollins in 1995), but he got a message from Amazon notifying him that the e book's purchase button has been yanked till he wi-fi it is formatting.

The problem? He had his desk of contents in the back of the e-book. as soon as he moved it, Amazon sent a message to everybody who had ever bought the 7451f44f4142a41b41fe20fbf0d491b7 making it sound like Mr. Williams had offered a poorly formatted version.

Later that month, Kindle directors published on Amazon forums about the organisation's table of contents coverage, writing, "some inside the network have contacted us about the sports of a small minority of publishers who may also try to inflate income or pages examine thru the use of diverse strategies, together with adding needless or perplexing links, misplacing the TOC [table of contents] or adding distracting content material."

After digging via the suppositions of diverse writers pointing palms at Amazon, it's clean to apprehend why placing a table of contents at the lower back may want to improve the corporation's ire, and the very truth that it has instituted a policy towards that practice suggests the suppositions are proper.

Amazon neither confirmed nor denied that its machine is getting gamed. "It's important to us to ensure that clients can agree with our sales' scores and that those ratings accurately reflect valid customer pastime," an Amazon spokesperson informed the Observer in an email. "so as now not to expose whatever to capability abusers, we don't talk the species-fics of the gear we use to check for abuse, and we are continuously operating to improve them."

Step 16: How to Hustle Kindle limitless

The hassle lies inside the workings of Amazon's Kindle unlimited provider, which gives readers unlimited access to greater than a million ebooks for $nine.99 according to month. As authors A.G. Riddle, Hugh Howey and Kristen Ashley have all informed us, this is a deal for avid readers, some of whom wi-finish a couple of e-books according to week. Plus, more than one authors have told us that being part of the Kindle limitless program has also multiplied their pro wireless, discoverability and readership.

Kindle unlimited authors receive a commission out of a pool of wireless installation by way of Amazon every month ($14.nine million in March 2016). Their cut of that pool is determined by way of the range of pages a reader reads of their ebooks, no longer by using the range of ebooks readers check out. top performers get a further boost of as lots as $25,000 in one month for being a pinnacle ten creator.

however, what if someone wirelesses a way to trick Amazon into believing that "readers" have examined heaps of pages when in reality they haven't examined any?

As writer Ann Christy wrote on her blog, "Scammers being scammers, they found out Amazon turned into lying very early on. Amazon couldn't inform what pages have been examining. They only knew the ultimate location you had been at within the e-book."

In other words: if a scam author publishes an e-book packed with wireless nonsense (maybe a mishmash of some thousand randomly picked pages from public domain websites), but then includes a hyperlink on the front that takes a Kindle limitless reader to the ultimate page, Amazon will check in that as though the consumer has "study" the entire e-book and pay the writer for heaps of pages analyzing that in no way happened.

In March, a German blog broke down a group of strategies for growing the numbers of pages study. for example, write a 100-web page book, then auto-translate it into one of a kind languages and invite your readers to click on through to the primary page in their native tongue. If 95 percent of your readers are English speakers, web page one could come after the Chinese, Italian and Pashto versions, then as quickly as they have got clicked to the primary English web page, Amazon thinks they have got study three hundred pages.

See how that works?

here's the good privacy information: Authors wouldn't be able to put up e-books that trick Amazon if its Kindles were virtually looking users study. if your tool has been timing how long it takes for you wireless a page, how regularly you appearance up phrases, cross back, skip forward and click on hyperlinks, Amazon could recognize you hadn't examined three,000 pages when you bought tricked into clicking to the give up. The scams work due to the fact all of the enterprises seem to understand is what web page a reader had open whilst she or he closes a virtual e-book.

earlier this month, writers (David Gaughran and Ms. Christy) broke down the natural scam state of affairs based totally on their very own studies within the Kindle store. right here's how every says it works: publish a Kindle unlimited e-book loaded with clicky phrases (as an aside, paranormal bear romance is a thing now), get click farms and paid reviewers to give it a gaggle of phony engagement in order that it rises up in the ranks after which positioned some form of gimmick at the front that hints readers into clicking to the lower back of the ebook. whilst readers near the crummy ebook in frustration, the scammer gets paid for a load of analyzing that never passed off.

Ms. Christy gives one example of an e-book she downloaded whose title key phrases consist of "Interracial Alpha Male being pregnant," although inside are pages and pages of textual content that don't make the experience (right here's a screenshot she made).

Step 17: What's Amazon doing?

In its response to the Observer, Amazon did not wi-fi the rip-off but said that it takes any gaming of its site several wirelesses. The fact is, the rip-off doesn't fee Amazon cash. It decides how huge the Kindle unlimited payout could be each month. Downloading bogus ebooks might mildly irritate Kindle limitless subscribers, but it doesn't cost them something either. so long as subscribers maintain their subscriptions, Amazon continues making a living and the scam doesn't cut into the corporation's wi-fi.

in the long run, although, if too many authors cease including accurate content material to the pool and too many readers wireless it polluted, that would alternate. And, the business enterprise has made some policy modiwiwireless that corroborate Mr. Gaughran and Ms. Christy's wi-findings. First, the aforementioned rule about setting tables of contents on the front.

2nd, Amazon has capped the Kindle limitless payout at 3,000 pages, which shows that the organization is aware that there are ebooks with inflated and phony web page counts.

On Mr. Gaughran's weblog, creator and writer Phoenix Sullivan shared her revel in looking a legitimate e-book she was promoting get crowded out of the top ratings via a hard and fast of e-books that in shape the scammer pro wirelessly. "I want to be the seller Amazon wishes me to be—exceptional, smart approximately promoting, a person who drives legitimate site visitor wireless to their site, a money-maker for us and them, and a cheerleader for their offerings," she writes. "Why do they make it so wi-fault?"

It's wi-difficult to imagine how Amazon can give you a restore that will hold scammers from siphoning cash out of the Kindle limitless pool, for now.

for instance, Mr. Gaughran points out that there's no correct way to flag suspicious e-books. "customer support levels at KDP are nonetheless unacceptable," he writes. "whilst there may be a severe or complex problem, KDP customer support can be awful. This has been an issue for years now and has by no means been properly addressed."

Ms. Christy shows a freeze on new debts and a more in-depth vetting system for brand new authors. but that would unfairly punish valid writers. Wikipedia uses wi-ficialwireless intelligence to flag terrible edits for humans to review. Why couldn't AI study to spot phony ebooks wi-fi junk? It's one of these group-American human beings and machines are suited to do collectively. Amazon might already be the use of robots to spot scammers, but we don't recognize.

It's a much higher plan to charge the child gadget overlords with scanning Mr. Bezos's literary inventory for garbage than it'd be to set the machines to watching humans as they examine.

Step 18: Publish

Subsequent you want to test the layout of the ebook. if you have a Kindle device, it's feasible to truly ship the report in your Kindle electronic mail cope with or switch it manually the use of a USB cable. rather, use the Kindle Previewer software to test thee-ebook on your computer.

If matters are searching good, it's time to hit the publish button. visit kdp.amazon.com, sign up the use of your Amazon credentials and upload the e-bookeeebook wi-documents (in case your book has photos, positioned the whole lot in one zip report.) You want to set the price of your e-book at this degree: Amazon will pay you 70% if your e-book's rate is $2.99 or higher, however for something less expensive, the royalty charge is only 35%.

the general workflow is extraordinarily person-pleasant, however, it's disappointing that Amazon expenses global clients a $2 Whispernet tax even if they use c084d04ddacadd4b971ae3d98fecfb2a (and now not 3G) to download the ebook. as a result, if you have set the e-book charge at $2.ninety nine, customers out of doors the U.S. would have to shell out $4.ninety nine, which is a damper for lower-priced ebooks.

once I wi-first uploaded the raw wi-fi to Kindle Publishing, it took some hours for the e-book to seem in Amazon's shop (a person possibly manually critiques the e-book, however, the technique is remarkably quick.) I made some corrections, re-uploaded the e-book and the up to date model also have become available in an hour or two. It doesn't get an awful lot less complicated wireless.

four Low-hazard ways to Generate Passive learning wireless and Make Your cash paintings wi-ficult for You

There are numerous notably simple methods to generate extra wealth that do not involve shady "get wealthy quick" schemes or heavy in advance investments. right here are a few recommendations and assets for constructing multiple streams of income and getting a higher rate of return on your cash.

The goal

Our goal right here is to position our cash to paintings in extra ways than one and also build additional streams of pro wireless so we get toward wi-financial freedom. The ideas right here won't make you right away rich, but they also won't require a variety of prematurely investment or threat.

Sheryl Schuff, a CPA, creator, and consultant who helps human beings start and manipulate online businesses, says growing multiple streams of wi-fits is virtually the brand new "activity protection."

if you have more than one sales streams, you may not be affected as tons with the aid of the lack of a purchaser, a product provider, or an affiliate dating.

further, having different wi-fi streams except your nine-to-5wireless job can restrict your wireless vulnerability if you lose your activity—it is one way to put together in case you assume you might lose your process.

how to prepare in case you assume you may Lose Your activity

in case you're beginning to get an unnerving feeling that your job is on the line, you can do loads...